THE ART
OF
DETACHMENT
IS
NOT
A LESSON OF
LETTING GO.

The Art Of Detachment

For the people who are somewhere in between healing.

The Art Of Detachment

A Poetry Collection

The art of detachment, is not a lesson of letting go

The Art Of Detachment

The art of detachment, is not a lesson of letting go,
Copyright © 2023

All rights reserved.

No part of this book may be reproduced, distributed, or transmitted in any form or b
any means including electronic, mechanical, photocopying, recording, or otherwise
without the prior written consent of the author.

Disclaimer:
This book contains explicit mature content and language.

Formatting, poems
cover and Illustration made by Madison

ISBN 978-1-7388770-1-0

Madison Farraway.
Canada, Ont.

Maddocuments.contact@gmail.com

The Art Of Detachment

Explaining the art of detachment

Understanding how to detach yourself is not just about letting go,
It is about understanding the root of the attachment, to better help yourself heal and become more aware of any issues or self- destructive acts your unconscious pain or hurt may be feeding.
Whether it is an attachment to a place, past or a person.
The art of detachment is learning how to emotionally detach from past trauma, relationships, grief, and substance abuse,
While healing and learning to love yourself too.

The Art Of Detachment

Contents

Where it began..9

It didn't start with you..........................39

A part of me died with you....................81

The art of detachment..........................117

The Art Of Detachment

The Art Of Detachment

The Art Of Detachment

Where It began.

The Art Of Detachment

I have always been unconventional and
I live within my head, my head only.
It's raw, it's loud, and it's invasive.
I'm not lonely, it's not empty, at least not within.
I have a set state of mind; it makes me, it breaks me.
It's just about suffocating, but I wouldn't change it. I love it.

I chew up every ounce of talk about terrible sex experiences,
and the way we didn't feel so ashamed.
I Laugh at the boys we used to love,
and the way we all wanted to die.
It gnawed at my soul as I watched her turn into everything she said she didn't want to be, it gets lonely and I feel so invasive.

But when we woke up together the morning after, to a disgusting house of ash and empty bottles, slowly to lose every sense of self I could get.
Breathing so deeply that my line of vision slightly moved.
As my body inhales and exhales, it feels as if the ground and walls were inhaling too.

The Art Of Detachment

I want to be loved, I don't need it to feel real, I don't need to feel whole.
It's disgusting, it's so unnerving.
It's like it may be the vein of the entirety of my existence;
and as I look back at the years I realize time flew by,
and I lived fast but don't we all.
Everyday that I lived felt like an entire lifetime.
Everyday I didn't feel that I was the same person
as I was the night before.
Time didn't feel like it moved, hours drag, my days blend together
and a sense of boredom consumed me.
Consuming every thought, every memory, consuming me entirely.
I attempt to distract this adolescence feeling,
a feeling of being utterly disconnected
from everyone and everything, a feeling of being unheard.
I'm passionate, I'm stubborn, I love and I hate.
I'm comparing this neutral state between such human antics.
This void is my consciousness.
I am unaware of the definition of contentment.
Satisfaction being a daydream consumed by boredom.
So how do I ever sustain satisfaction within a twenty-four
hour period? My mind is in twenty-four different places.

The Art Of Detachment

It's quiet, but it creeps up on you slowly.
Like cracks in a haunted house.
But nothing looks too different,
at least not from a first glance.
As the days longing, you begin to
not only hear, but you see it now too.
Soon enough, alarms will begin to go off.
The first picture lights up
and you watch as you know there is nothing
you can do, once it spreads.
You wonder how you could have been so blind to it all,
you see when you grow up in home in flames,
you begin to think the whole world is on fire.

- A broken home

The Art Of Detachment

Talking to you is like walking on eggshells,

but I love it when you make me cry or even better,

when you make me laugh.

I adore when you scream at me

I go to bed with a sore throat and wake up with puffy eyes most nights.

I love when you treat me as nothing,

I'll love whatever you decide to give me,

whatever I'm lucky enough to have.

Last night I fell asleep with my

fingers crossed, I pleaded my sheets to hug me and hold me,

like you once did. I woke fingers still crossed,

blood bathed sheets only to wake up to the same mess,

I went to sleep in.

The Art Of Detachment

"Maybe I'll never be good enough for you"

I don't feel that I'll ever be good enough for you.
Almost as if you saw yourself within the reflection of my eyes.
The thought of me having to go through a life without the
experiences you lived through didn't sit right within
I suppose. I don't feel I'll ever be good enough for you.
I am exhausted with what I see, love me, hate me
It all looks the same. Eventually that list could fill an entire book.
I alter my image to intertwine with yours,
maybe then I could be good enough for you.
Trying to prove my words with a letter of grades
but I guess I'm just tired of feeling like nothing to you.

The Art Of Detachment

It wasn't the silence that chipped away at my self-esteem,
It was the absence of your love but a feeling that is no longer there.
The feeling left at the exact moment you changed,
the moment you decided to adapt yourself, for another.

The Art Of Detachment

You want me to tell you
that them loving each other
was going to hurt them more than letting go.
They didn't know how to love,
they bonded over the lack of love they weren't shown as children,
but in the end this broke them.
she couldn't love him, she didn't know how to love.
He didn't know how to love, so he could differ when to stop.

- Lack of love

The Art Of Detachment

They told me I was mature for my age,
what they didn't realize was my childhood
was stolen, and I was forced to grow up.
Spoon fed responsibility and independence,
and I'm not talking about dishes and setting
tables for dinner.
Alone and lost.
Made to swallow the rage because boys simply
"do not know better".
Hungry just to be heard and understood.
Sharpening my tongue to only bite on my own words
because it seems unseemly to lie bleeding.
but, I was only a child.

The Art Of Detachment

I want to make and create something so big
something permanent, something worthwhile.
I've felt a sense of pride over my accomplishments
a sense of accomplishment over small wins, but this fades.
I choke on the thought of being utterly
consumed by the thought not only being free, but feeling free too.

They asked where I went, what happened to me.
They say they don't recognize me anymore but,
all I ever wanted was to be free, free of all.
I need to experience everything life has to offer,
to be free of an endless cycle our world is consumed by.
A new chapter, maybe a new story.
Something to give.

The Art Of Detachment

If I served my pain on a plate and asked you would feast on it, you would be unable to.

You see, you spent your entire life swallowing your own darkness you no longer want mine.

Much like a cigarette we know it is bad but one way or the other some, end up consuming it becoming an addiction.

So as I attempt to serve my love, asking you to feast,

I console my own heart as it returns back to me empty.

You suffocated the child deep within and never mourned the loss of that child.

- Generational Trauma

The Art Of Detachment

Maybe it was the 4th,
or maybe the 14th.
It is unclear, but what is clear is it was some sick fucking crime.
Telling me to touch him there, whilst he touched me everywhere, it is unclear.

But I learned when I was 12, women are objects, and nothing more.
Told to dress and act a certain way.
We live in a world where sometimes no means go.
But I shouldn't have worn what I did, and I should have stayed sober.
I mean even though It haunts my dreams.
Shoving that bottle in my face then shoving himself into my personal space has left me uneasy.

The Art Of Detachment

I never told anyone.
I sat there in silence most nights painting upon my body,
a body I call a canvas, While I burn within.

I never told anyone the way I drank wasn't
because I was out of control, the way you thought I was.
It was because I was hurt and unable to deal with my emotions
in any other manner.
But I wished for answers, god did I wish for answers.
I wished someone were to understand that this was my cry for help.

- Don't be blind to those around you

The Art Of Detachment

At the ripe age of 12,
he remembers the feeling of his first time.
His first time but not his last.

The first time where his mind begins to drift off,
Sitting there with the lights off.
The tingly feeling begins to set in.
The voices of his false reality begin to make their appearance
as he is vulnerable,
scared,
lost.
His throat begins to close
his mouth begins to dry,
and he sinks into his sheets.
He's paralyzed and disturbed,
but that was only the beginning

The Art Of Detachment

A cold dark morning, snow covering the grounds,
the world went quiet and you laid there, lifeless.

As the drugs began to run through your blood, you drank
And Your smile began to fade to nothing.
Exhausted and numb you lay there lifeless but breathing.

The world went quiet, dark and empty.
I then realized, a world that felt lonely was lonely.

The Art Of Detachment

A warm night of July, 2018.

The worry and fear began to take place as he spent most nights consumed by thought not so much of what could be, but what was.

They try to fill that young boy's head

that it wasn't something to be concerned about.

But how could he not be worried that the person

that was supposed to love, and hold him when he had a nightmare,

caused the nightmare in an attempt to leave him.

The Art Of Detachment

It seems my whole life I've been uncomfortable.

My whole life, I've been uneasy, I choke on the discomfort of being here.

I sat at the end of the bed, picking the scabs from my arms

as I watch you putter around in hopes to find the only thing

you've searched your entire life to find, but failed to do so.

I watch the day turn to night, in hopes for change

only to be consumed by the thought of it.

I fear the feeling of contentment as if I ever find it

it will be stripped head to toe from me.

The Art Of Detachment

Our world, our home

provided with a service of protection.

Unable to identify the protection that is given.

Given more information to the hands of leaders that are

supposed to protect and give but, they take and give nothing to return.

Given one job to protect, given one responsibility

but failed to an ounce of that.

A file, only a file that was denied to be made because

the little boy was unable to speak, unable to make a sound.

If handed you a book of evidence and a video you would

have turned your back and said

nothing could be done, nothing to prove, nothing I can do.

- A corrupted system

The Art Of Detachment

He hated me

but I hated him a bit more so it was okay.

What we had was never full,

it was never complete or whole.

But even a dead flower looks beautiful

in a ice cold desert of nothing

The Art Of Detachment

She carves out every logistic part of her,
why you ask?

Everything that was awful fuels
a short lived feeling, she calls peace.
The sense of torment drowns herself in a calm.

Water and fire, good and bad they are elementary terms,
the translation meets the same definition.

You asked how she translates the most recognizable elements
to meet the same end?
she says stay long enough and I'll show you.

- How I turn a good to evil

The Art Of Detachment

And it rained yesterday, it poured, it was dark.
I wasn't alive yesterday, no.
I woke up dead with a pit in my stomach, hate in my heart.
I felt as if I was drowning in the pit of my past,
I felt gross and I was gloomy.
A hate for myself that was so calculated,
so rational and well thought out.
A dread for the hours that lay before me,
could destroy the life that lays ahead of me

The Art Of Detachment

As I spoke to him, I began stepping into the role of you.
only a role in a play I didn't sign up for.
A role that the one that did sign up for no longer wanted.
So I cooked the healthiest boxed food I could find.
Picking out a meal to meet all the nutrients you need
and topped with vegetables.
when I had had to step into positions of care,
for those who no longer wanted to
It is easy to abandon and the most healed parts of me,
the parts that are fluent in the language of boundaries.

The Art Of Detachment

Eight

That is when she began to pick out her own clothes
and pack her own bag.
That is when she realized nothing would ever be the same.
She was going to be leaving soon,
she wasn't ready to grow up
but she had to.

Twelve

She began to worry about all she could not control,
when she began to hear all the voices in her head.

Fourteen

Is when she began to try and fill that void.
She began to consume anything and everything
that was accessible to her.
You see nothing ever did fill that part of her,
And nothing ever would because the only thing that could
was you.

The Art Of Detachment

I've turned your idea of your love into hate.
I hate being loved by your filtered chosen words.
I am raw and harsh, you looked sick
as I choked up an attempt for an explanation.
I wanted to be ravished by your love
I wanted it to tear me apart, as if it hadn't already.
I wanted to be devoured to the bone,
I wanted your love to be irrational.
To lose sleep over something, to finally not in vain.
I will never be enough for you,
my face emptied and I choked up a smile.
as if my dimorphous expression could ever make you
love me as painfully as I do.

- I wanted to feel your love, I wanted you to love me

The Art Of Detachment

I don't know why you wasted your love on him,
Why you couldn't have given it to me.
You fed him more then he ever deserved,
and left me starving.
You left me relentlessly begging for your love,
watching as you take my plate to fill his.
I only wanted your love, I only wanted you to let him go
but you never did.
So we suffered.
You hungering for his love, Whilst I hunger for yours.

The Art Of Detachment

I've always wondered what you
looked like without alcoholism written upon you.

- What did you look like before?

The Art Of Detachment

When I was a child I didn't think two birthdays

ever was better than one whole birthday.

I was belittled, the divorce of one's parents is overlooked,

it is normalized.

They don't tell you about the arguments,

nor the guilt of having to pick a parent to stand beside.

I can not bring the words to explain

other than it feels like a piece of you,

is dead inside.

The Art Of Detachment

His words, his actions, his eyes full of hatred.
He hated that I knew everything he so deeply tried to hide.
He hated that I owned that power over him,
I never did anything with that knowledge.
Even through all his words of anger.
They say blood is everything, but blood doesn't mean family
and you can burn this book but my words will live on until they no longer remember.

The Art Of Detachment

The Art Of Detachment

The Art Of Detachment

It didn't Start Because of you.

The Art Of Detachment

A silent torture, where the only real evidence resides within.
A collection of invisible scars within the mind
deeper than the ones that lay upon my body.
Carving out all the logistic parts of you,
and replacing it with doubt.
Silent movements to get yourself out, but it is a vicious loop.
A loop that goes round and round, again and again here we go,
the same old routines of you showing remorse and guilt.
Followed up with a song of an excuse
making sure it is better than the last,
just enough for me to cave into a false act of love.
I am not a slave to your words.
I write my own narrative, evolving straight lines.

The Art Of Detachment

What is it about the mold of summer and winter?
I dwindle, I shine.
Autumn and spring let me get a glimpse of the air, there is a set of
thoughts and feelings. It makes me, it breaks me
it consumes me, it makes me whole, they craft and they mold me.

The seasons, the time of year create a meek set of choices,
it glosses over me. The time of year I can cruise the roads,
and walk the beach at night, the time of year that I feel contentment.
Winter it gorges me, it drains me, it's so intense I fall and I grow,
but it's the time of the year I seem to grow the most.

The Art Of Detachment

I cannot get used to being here,

It feels so uneasy, so unsettling, so unfamiliar

but I know I could walk these roads blindfolded.

My inner child struts around

in hopes to find the security she never got.

Hungry to be heard and feel loved.

It's sad and beautiful really but it makes me sick to think of.

The Art Of Detachment

Honestly,
I wonder if you truly are blind
to the pain you caused me.

The Art Of Detachment

"You are not a home.
 People are not supposed to be homes."

And they confused me as a child,
because people say,
family is everything, so I made a home out of you.
But you are not supposed to make a home out of people
at least not when they can walk in and out at their convenience.

The Art Of Detachment

I emptied my soul so there was room for yours.

I thought about you as I drove down that old road, it was cold

and dark but I suffered a slow transition from love to hate.

The balance of this life,

that I would throw away for you.

Is like A bright orange and a rotten apple. It is the same.

My blood spills on the floor of the bathroom,

the way you told me you hated me last night

has my heart and stomach intertwined;

it cuts off receptors in my mind.

The way you told me you loved me in the morning

left a flat toned, blank expression and

it is all I see in the reflection of the mirror.

The Art Of Detachment

Your entire self worth has been based on your academic ability.
You treat us like we are beat up old toys, if we don't succeed.
Raise your hand until it goes numb,
You are a child and you don't know what is best for you.
Sacrifice the entirety of my
mental well being to show you I can make and take.
I can draw outside the lines and still make a name,
if you think this is real learning,
your whole life you have been robbed.

- A Corrupt school system

The Art Of Detachment

You wouldn't have spoken to me again,

had I done that to you.

The Art Of Detachment

The world feels off.
My mind, my line of vision is off,
I feel like i'm floating outside
of my body looking down on myself
but everything is still.

The Art Of Detachment

I am not being dramatic, I am terrified of my own
and the places it takes me to.
Time blends together,
the feeling of running to a vacant destination too long.

Trying to control your breathing while no one notices .
Worrying about what was to come,
Your mind, so full your eyes become blurry.
Oh god and did she bite her cheeks if you watch her carefully.

Sometimes I skip sleep because my head already feels washed.
Sometimes I skip sleep because I dream of time not being lost.
Anxiety is like a roommate that won't sleep nor tell you why.
This roommate is only used to taking time,
but you can not kill her because she is a part of me.

- *my anxiety and I.*

The Art Of Detachment

And as I drown my heart in a bottle I found in the cupboard,
I realize this is the feeling I've been looking for,
this is the feeling I've been searching for.
But the thing is I don't feel anything.
I remember as a little child I always said no, that will never be.
But now it is, I've turned into everything I said I didn't want to be.

- I found peace within your bottle

The Art Of Detachment

Three seconds that all it was three seconds,
but three seconds that she didn't want,
Three seconds that she said no.
Three seconds that,
you gutted her like she was nothing but a dummy.

The Art Of Detachment

He waited years to find the person he used to be.
Years to get those two seconds of nothingness,
years to get back the confidence back he once had as a little boy
years to feel "normal" again.
Until one night
he did it, he let go.
He let go of all worry, he let go of everything.
Any care, everything was gone.
and it was the best he had ever felt.
The shy person, he had know for as long as he could remember
was gone,
the lost, insecure person was gone.
He felt good
he felt confident
he had found the feeling he had been searching for what felt
like a lifetime's worth of time.
He felt the feeling of that 10 year old
the little boy inside him came back.

- The first time

The Art Of Detachment

Drugs there addictive,

numbing, they give a sense of a false reality.

Sometimes the best experiences they give to humans…

and some of the worst.

I mean they were great that one Friday night…right?

And the next, then Saturday too.

but It's only a weekend thing,

but when the "weekend" thing starts to become a little more

than a weekend thing. Your family and loved ones

begin to notice a change and your grades drop,

and your motivation begins to fade away.

People ask questions, so you distance yourself.

Because it's only a weekend thing and I don't need to worry.

And there my friends.

but, when you're alone and scared,

who do you call when you push everyone away?

alone and cold,

who do you look to when no one will look at you?

The Art Of Detachment

I often think about how life could have been.
How I would have been,
had not endured the pain I endured.
How would we all be?

The Art Of Detachment

I am l given the sudden subtle relief,
relieved that I've shown a small sliver of what I am capable of.
As if they l know what this means to me, I mean as if the way that old man told me I had something special was something we haven't all heard.
My whole life I've been shut down and I was just relieved I could finally prove I was worth something.
The only person that knows how badly I want to bare my soul is me.
This is something I had to do to gain a little relief and this relief fades.
I am empty. All I want to accomplish is not familiar with me yet, there will never be enough life for me. The instinct of greed is so gremmie, I hate the way the way it looks on me, yet I want to scream on a stage so they all see me and see how badly I want this how i need this,
I caused myself great pain because without it I could not be here.

The Art Of Detachment

"You can not be loved until you love yourself" said Nizar Qabbani
But for him, he found love without the love for himself.
May or may it not be forever, there will always be a part of him
that will remember the time, he would have done anything for it.

- The First High

The Art Of Detachment

He never liked the idea of drinking,

It never really caught his eye.

Until he took that sip,

he realized he could hide from the feelings of grief.

He could run from it,

It feared him the thought of him losing someone

so close to him.

It feared him knowing that person, his person

was soon leaving him.

So he drank,

It numbed him,

It was like a bandaid to him,

but he could only drink for so long.

The Art Of Detachment

I see a person depersonalized.
That's me at the table, I am an illusion.
I am out of place, the days blending together, The days are longing,
I sit here watching a movie, only a movie
I do not feel like I'm a casted in.
Are the people in the movie aware of how little I feel to be my own being? I'm at a party, only a party I don't want to be at.
Anxiety being the first cousin visiting from out of the country, bringing derealization, feeling obligated to bring to the party. I am the party.
I don't want to be here, I am out of place, I am out of body.
I am watching my movie, but I am not in.
This sickness has its claws intertwined around my mind, and so deeply within.

- Derealization

The Art Of Detachment

He sat there,
alone,
cold,
and thought to himself.
If I didn't take beer,
If I didn't pick up that cigarette,
would I be someone else?
Would I be farther than where I am now?
If I had not let my worries I made within my head
control me, would I be different?

The Art Of Detachment

And as your path crossed mine, You painted a smile on my face.

You marking a place where you've been,

you cover the markings I painted within my body,

you place a bandaid on wounds you did cause.

And I began to make a home out of you,

a home you could knock down whenever you pleased,

only because I thought about you a little too much in my spare time.

The Art Of Detachment

For him to tell her that children don't feel pain,
was like him saying children don't bleed.
He says this as the blood drips down from her wrist,
If children don't bleed, I guess adults don't cry, she says.

The Art Of Detachment

You drain the blood from my veins,
Sucking the life from my soul.
You pray to me like I belong to you,
never being freed from your toxic cycle.
You take my successes and define them as your own,
You drag me down so low,
to depths many people never experience in a lifetime.
I am not a hobby you get to pick up and drop, Whenever you see fit.
1 am not your punching bag, I am not your employee, that you can
instruct and manipulate. I am just another human trying to get through
this so-called life.

The Art Of Detachment

I found the peace in art at at young age,
painting , drawing, writing.

I'd tear part my most vulnerable parts of me to
use my body as a canvas.
Painting away, until I've carved my own art gallery.
Sometimes a little to passionate
but after all maybe twelve was a little young
to become an artist.

- My perfect canvas

The Art Of Detachment

I have a void within me
A hole in my chest, in my heart.
I have a wall that you built for me, and it stands up against me.
I am unable to scream I am unable to leave, I am stuck here
and you built this wall, you made this void,
and now no amount of love could fill.

The Art Of Detachment

Love and hate truly are close, I didn't realize till I met you.
You treated me like nothing, you tied me up
unable to do anything.
But despite it all I still love you.

The Art Of Detachment

"Maybe the moon is beautiful only
because it is far away"

- Mahamoud Darwish

The Art Of Detachment

Nothing is more consistently enjoyable
then like eating your favorite food
while watching your favorite movie.
It's your favorite so it never gets old,
always being as good as the first time,
making you feel real again, making you feel whole.
Almost like everything could be perfect again but it is not,
giving up your other half to live a mundane, melancholic life.
A trap but a beautiful one you say.

The Art Of Detachment

He talks to people around trying to find comfort
and the answers within.
Mainly girls, he figured they would be there to comfort him
in a way that could understand him better, but it didn't help.
He would hide his emotions,
from everyone,
even himself.
he would put on a fake smile,
laugh at jokes that weren't funny.
He knew keeping those feelings inside weren't good,
but the thought of others knowing feared him.
What he didn't fear was a blade to his wrist.
It gave him comfort,
It gave him relief.
He found satisfaction watching the blood
drip from his wrist,
he found reason.
And In those moments nothing else mattered to him.

The Art Of Detachment

One hit, one line, one bump

He deeply thinks within how disappointed
she would be of him might she ever find out,
all the conversations, all the promises and the lies he tells.

Two hits

"I wish he would see what he's done to me" She says

Three hits

He starts to forget
her voice,
her smile,
and her laugh

Four hits

He laughs and laughs
"She doesnt matter, she's nothing,"
he says, until the comedown.

- Nohappyendings

The Art Of Detachment

My entire life I have felt something has been missing.
My entire life I have been insearch of a constant murmur
that sits in the back of my head.
My entire life I have tried to fill a void.
Only to come to realize the void I was trying to fill, was you.

I was trying to fill the lack of love, support and empathy
I searched my entire lifetime to find,
but I failed to do so, and I will never be able to fill that.

The Art Of Detachment

You deprive yourself of love

and as much as you think people don't see it they do.

I see the way you sleep the hours away,

I see the way you burn bridges of the people you love.

You deprive yourself of love

I get it, you're scared of what is within.

You think you are being quiet

but your footsteps are loud in an empty house.

Butterflies don't see their beauty but I do, and I see yours.

The Art Of Detachment

As a child, setting my world up Perfectly to my invision
of "a perfect life" only to walk all over it.
Breaking my world, my envision, my innocence.
I guess I enjoyed the sharp pains when stepping on the
odd one wrong. So childish, they took it as maturity.

Maybe I enjoyed the pain to unconsciously drown out the voices
of my "unrealistic life" I intended for myself
or maybe my unrealistic feelings.
But as time went on those
voices only seemed to get louder to move my line of vision.

I witness the earth move with my inhalation
It pinched my nerves. Why does it feel out of reach to find myself,
but it is suffocatingly boring to be free.

The Art Of Detachment

I don't feel anything.

A cloud I feel but it is flight or fight and this feeling is flight.

As maybe the emotional needs needed to be met as a child weren't there.

Dissociated for years using to cope to repress those feelings, because they were unable to be met, instead of voicing them.

The Art Of Detachment

I hate writing these words, nothing has changed.
You didn't change, you haven't changed.
I write lines that I wish you see,
I tell a story that I'd wish you would hear.
But I know when you tell me your sorry,
I fall back into the same place I was with you.

The Art Of Detachment

The scariest part about having suicidal thoughts is over time,
they begin to feel more and more like the only solution.
Like the best solution.
Every memory,
every thought,
every reason starts to disappear.

The Art Of Detachment

The feeling of being a burden never fades,
you see if he leaves the pain doesn't come with him.
It moves on to you,
so as he pictures it, he pictures you.

- The feeling of being a burden never ends

The Art Of Detachment

You don't know how deeply you hurt me.

My soul nor my body.

Instead of texting when you need,

or exchanging a smile, I have to act as if nothing ever existed.

The Art Of Detachment

For being the joyful, loving person I can be, I am empty.

I have a happy personality, with a sad soul and sure

I'm not always joyful, and happy or give the

right love when it's needed, but I work hard and I care.

I glow when I do, I study business and write.

I'll give the clothes off my back for you,

I have a certain quality. I know it and you know it too.

But this quality is what turns my admiration to hate.

A quality of confidence accompanied by self awareness

The Art Of Detachment

Obsessed with love,

a hopeless romantic,

chasing after any high, and disappointed in the comedown.

When reality sets in you add another name to the list,

a hopeless romance.

- A high

The Art Of Detachment

A Part Of Me Died With You.

The Art Of Detachment

"A Part Of Me Died With You"

When you died a part of me died with you.
It doesn't feel right that I'm here, and your not,
It doesn't feel right that my heart beats and yours doesn't.
Now you're here and I'm not,
my heart beat for you, yours didn't beat for mine
now you're here and I'm not.

The Art Of Detachment

Grief isn't a long lost cousin visiting from out of town. Grief a neighborhood friend, only a neighborhood friend that is too close to the touch. A neighborhood friend that is familiar, almost too familiar with me. See they don't tell you that grief isn't just about losing someone you love. They don't tell you mourning a person doesn't always mean they leave from within this life, it also can mean they just leave from your life.

- And you Left

The Art Of Detachment

You gave me your hand at birth, but unbeknownst to me
I cannot find it anymore. You made those promises
but were those promises kept?

I remember your bright dresses,
Your hair flowed in the wind, and your skin glowed.
But I don't remember that anymore, it all happened so fast it seemed
I hear you, only I can't see you anymore.
It's dark here now, cold.
See you've fallen but when did you plan on getting up?

The Art Of Detachment

Every day,
every sleepless night
I wonder why I am not enough

I try to think of any reason,
any thought,
but maybe no words are better than an explanation.

The Art Of Detachment

You took something human out of me that night,
You took a part of me that was supposed to be with me forever.
The water has made an exit and it is dry here now.
I am cold to the touch, and I hate being cold.

- Numb

The Art Of Detachment

There was a lot you could have paid more attention to.
Things were happening.
Stuff happened but you weren't there.

- I needed you

The Art Of Detachment

Your love is uneven.

You have me map out the stars to predict your tide.

Some days you're shores dry, others I drown myself in

what you were not what you are.

You give me an expiration date but don't identity when it is,

so you set me to fly but give no time to learn how to dive.

- You set me to fly without giving me wings.

The Art Of Detachment

You melt my confidence away with every ugly word
like a burning candle,
but when you burn a candle for so long it grows to become empty.
I pressed my brain to two clouds,
you are a boiling pot filled to the rim to any excuse
you could overflow.

The Art Of Detachment

Every friday, every month at the same time 12:15 PM.
he was called to talk, and they listened but only
because they have to. Eventually he realized they didn't care,
they didn't want the best, they sat in that chair
for one thing and one thing only he says.
So he began to lose the release of talking,
and began to find his release within something new…

The Art Of Detachment

How loud did I have to scream
for you to hear me?

The Art Of Detachment

I hurt as I see you dissociate,

it will never get easier, you claim you don't want this,

so I leave or walk beside you.

we travel down our separate paths

and I hope it is the last.

The Art Of Detachment

Tomorrow will begin and I won't be there.
Understand that it was my calling,
I was taken by the hand, my time was up.
But at the expense to leave behind everything and everyone
I yearned all my life for.
But I walked through the fates of those doors
only to feel more at home, then I knew I could.
So when tomorrow begins, and I'm not there,
don't think I am gone.
If I cross your mind, remember,
I'll walk beside you when you need me.

- A letter for you

The Art Of Detachment

It's 2:46 AM, the world is quiet and everyone is asleep.
You feel the vibrations of the AC travel within the house you called home, but maybe not so "home" anymore?
you move with every inhale and exhale
But as you laid there, listing to her gurgle the last bit of life she had the world went quiet, well your world went quiet.
And as you lay there listing to her last breaths
knowing that there would be nothing in the world to ever compare to her. You lay there choking on the thoughts of what is about to come, and you know there is nothing that could be done.
You lay there as your body begins to shiver and the goosebumps begin to take over every inch of your body head to toe. It's 2:55 am the voice don't stop, the sound of choking on saliva does not stop, but as you lay there waiting for time to pass focusing on the sound of the ac run throughout the house, trying to control your inhalation with every exhale. The phone begins to ring but you can't move, you can't get up, you're paralyzed by the thought of what is, and what could have been but there is nothing you could've done.

The Art Of Detachment

I would hand you every fuckin piece of me.
Everything I have, stripped down to the bone,
to hear you laugh like you once did.

The Art Of Detachment

It is my fault.
I knew your promises were empty.
The weight of your pain, and the alcohol that failed
to make it go away. I knew that your drunk heartwarming
Speeches of I love yous, wouldn't matter as you awaken.
But I was lonely, so I wrap myself within your lies
Pretending they were the truth. But as the cotton turned
to a suit of needles, I was disregarded.
The blood ran off my skin, and the ink left a smudge on the paper
of what could have been.
I am nothing but blurred words and veins,
and I don't know who is to blame.

The Art Of Detachment

Every now and then,
he thinks about changing his hair.
Maybe the flowers will soon grow out of his eyes instead of hers.
Maybe if he changes his hair again,
he will be able to act like he did before.

- Will my hair change me?

The Art Of Detachment

I wrapped myself in a blanket
pressed my hand upon my chest,
I felt my heartbeat for the first time in what felt like hours
but I couldn't differ.
The days of longing nights are never ending

I closed my eyes picturing a smile,
that could ease my pain
but I still feel empty.

It's been 517 days.
How many more
till the pain subsides ?

The Art Of Detachment

I never said goodbye, he says.
"That is what eats through my flesh right through to my heart"

But you see he didn't feel that cold november morning
not until a few weeks or months, then after a bit of time had
passed he realized that she wasn't coming back.
She wasn't going to be there to give her advice to him,
she wasn't going to be there to love or hold,
she was gone forever for now.
That is what broke him, that she was no longer here.

The Art Of Detachment

You placed a band-aid over wounds you did not cause to
rip off at your own convenience.
But most heartbreaking part of this,
no one will ever be you.

The Art Of Detachment

You're here but you've been gone for years.
And I wish I could have done more, but I was only a child.
I've walked these roads blind, because you weren't here

- I miss you

The Art Of Detachment

And as I say my last goodbye to you, you're not gone but
you have been consumed by all you preached you hated.
Everything you said you weren't going to be,
I've watched your entire self drift away day by day, minute by minute

The Art Of Detachment

Every towel in this bathroom is white.
The one that hangs behind the door left to dry.
And the two I leave on the counter for after the shower,
much like you used to do.
The bath water is too hot, I'm lightheaded
but I sit here, I drown myself in the thought
of what is, and what is no longer .
I'm here, and your there and I replay the sound of your voice,
the the touch of your hands and the feeling of your love
I can no longer hear you, I no longer feel you
you're no longer here.
I lay here dead in your absence
marking the place of where you once laid.
and for the first time ever, I wanted there to be an afterlife.

The Art Of Detachment

Though she lied there, still on the cold floor again
splitting open her stomach, her heart and all that was left of her
I watch as my spine splits open my back
and I'm stopped dead in my tracks as blood poured out,
but at least she got her happy ending right
or though she thought.

The Art Of Detachment

And I love you, I loved you.

You made me laugh on days I didn't remember how to.

I watch your soul fade, I watched you die

I watched you burn yourself away.

You made me sit there and watch you kill yourself knowing,

there was nothing I could do

Why,

Why did you do that?

The Art Of Detachment

Now that you're gone,
I reach instead my chest to hold onto the pieces of you
that made a home within.
Now that you're gone my face has wrinkled a bit from closing
my eyes to get a glimpse of your face.
They say the best way to move on is to go through
but I didn't think I would have to be here without you.
I don't know what is worse than knowing what was.
Even if you weren't in the whole story, I re-read the old chapters
to pretend that you were.
(I don't know why forever wasn't in the story.)

The Art Of Detachment

I'm sorry for not giving you the love you need,
I'm sorry for making you feel as nothing,
I'm sorry for not hugging you tighter,
I'm sorry for not telling you I loved you.

The Art Of Detachment

Grief screams were louder

when he sat in your empty room alone.

It is heavier to carry the weight of an absence alone, he says.

- no one prepares you for grief

The Art Of Detachment

Come back, as a shadow, as a ghost.
It doesn't matter just dont let me forget
the feeling of grief from you.
Because grief is all I have left,
grief gives me the sliver of the feeling that you are still here.
I find myself holding my breath because I'm afraid I will lose
whatever I have left of you with every exhale.
Let me mourn every second of every day we are apart.

- Awaken the grief

The Art Of Detachment

You can smoke,
and you can drink till you pass out

You can contine to slowly kill yourself but you know you won't forget the sound of their laugh when you awaken.

The Art Of Detachment

I crave you, the same way I crave summer in the winter.
I crave you like a ice cream on a hot day
but, it's only good at first, because if you wait to long
it gets messy and no matter how many napkins
you have, no amount could clean up that mess.

The Art Of Detachment

Learning detachment isn't a lesson of letting go.
It is a lesson of understanding,
that you were never mine
to keep,
convert,
or own.

The Art Of Detachment

"Do not base your entire self worth and happiness
in the hands of someone else, you will eventually lose yourself"

Something I've heard one too many times but
the absence of you seems to be the only reason for my unhappiness.
I do not recognize my reflection in a mirror as my own anymore.
You took me with you before I could get to know myself
So where do I go when nowhere feels like home without you?

The Art Of Detachment

You aren't taught about grief or how to deal with it, but what he learned through the journey of life was, that to come to realize those grieving emotionally don't come when you plan nor want. They come in the most unexpected moments.
Most times people see the significance of a loss.
A loss that seemed so big to you seems so little to them.
He finds that when one loses someone, you are better to prepare yourself when you get a chance to say goodbye, because when you can't it is harder to accept and acceptance is apart of healing so when you can't understand nor accept such a traumatic event
how does one move on from such a loss,
a loss that people did not find significant but you?

The Art Of Detachment

The Art Of Detachment

The Art Of Detachment.

The Art Of Detachment

And as you heal, Short text messages will no longer feel hateful.
As the realization you were never at fault begins to grow,
not every time you hear of people partying
you will connect it to something emotional.
Not every time someone cries you will think of the time
you had to wipe their eyes before your own,
Those apologies never felt right anyway.
Someday someone will tell you, love is what you deserve
instead of holding onto that hope on your own.
Don't speak to yourself unless you would say it
to a child version of you.
That is why you should care for the child you once were because
healing means becoming the parent you always needed.

The Art Of Detachment

The hard truth behind healing, is it is not linear.
It is lonely and raw.
Some days you will wake up feeling full, feeling at peace.
Then the next day, feeling like you're right back
at where you began.
Healing isn't linear, you will be tested, you will have set backs
and you will be lonely.
Healing is growing
healing is learning.
There will always be times where you sure it is over, but it isn't
Healing is growth,
and we are always growing,
so remember why you started.

The Art Of Detachment

You wonder why I left, why I walked out and why I didn't look back.
Because I loved myself more than the idea of your love.
I remembered I didn't need you to give me something,
I could give myself
I don't need your filtered words of false love.
I don't need you to feel loved.

The Art Of Detachment

Stop saying that the trauma you endured made you a better person,
that the trauma made you who you are,
that it carved and molded you to be better.
It was not necessary, you would have been just as compassionate and empathetic. You were beautiful before it just as you are reading this.
So don't say that it carved you into a better individual,
because that implies that it needed to happen, that you deserved it.
You didn't,
You didn't deserve that.
Those events did not alter your character,
you were perfect before it all.

The Art Of Detachment

I have this theory
you don't ever know someone,
You couldn't ever truly know someone.
People show you what they want you to see
and people tell you what they want you to hear.
Whether their purposely holding that information or just things they
forget about along the way. Everything within their life
is what makes them who they are.
It's impossible for them to tell you their entire life story.
From suppressed memories, the first day of school because for most
people that day is blurry, but it all adds to who they are.
So from sepressed childhood trauma or memories that is what
build them, and if they don't know how could you.
With this I don't think anyone ever truly knows themselves .
How do you ever truly know someone who doesn't know
who they are, or why they act curtain ways?

The Art Of Detachment

If they cared, they wouldn't have done what they did,
If they cared they wouldn't have put themselves in a position to lose you.
They wouldn't have left you wondering where you fit into their puzzle.
They would have known where your puzzle piece fit.
Their silence tells you everything you need to know.

- Their silence was clear

The Art Of Detachment

You learn everything you need to know by observing,
reading people like the pages of this book. Flipping through
Every movement,
every smile,
every emotion.
Understanding strangers without exchanging a single word with them, but yet I understand them. I feel the heaviness that lays within their eyes, I've experienced the weight of such a smile, I see the scars they attempt to hide, It is clear.
I see their motives through movements.

-The art of psychology through the eyes of an empath

The Art Of Detachment

She never called,

she never texted,

she never showed up.

And at some point along the way it stopped hurting as much.

Because, when you expect the sky to darken before it rains,

you are no longer surprised when it does.

- Acceptance is the first step to healing

The Art Of Detachment

From the outside, I'm a strong independent young woman
but somewhere deep down is a scared little girl
that feared most nights,
because she didn't know what was to come.
A little girl that was desperate to not only be loved to feel loved.
Until one day the outside began to seep through, to my mind
right into my blood and through my veins,
to give the little girl what she needed.

- Be who you needed as a child

The Art Of Detachment

Learn to make peace with the things
you don't talk about.

The Art Of Detachment

For as long as I wished,
I wished for you.

The Art Of Detachment

You hold all the power to your healing,
no one can change your thoughts, you can not change
the actions of others around you.

People can help you along the way
but at the end of the day,
It is only you who can change your perception of the world.

The Art Of Detachment

Become aware of your strengths and weaknesses. Understand where you can change and make improvements to be at peace with your weaknesses. Validate your own experiences and emotions, because at the end of the day you only have you.

The Art Of Detachment

My anger built up in a quiet way but it was loud
if you looked close enough.
A messy room, messy texts
I'd never let you know how you hurt me,
the kind of person who thinks it is better to be quite, so they
don't know they have the power over you to cause hurt.
That is probably not a good trait.
So I didnt let it out, I let it seep through my bones,
I took your words and carved them along my skin,
as if you were my burden to carry.
I am not unlovable. I am not a failure with nothing to say.
You didn't neglect me emotionally, you just left me behind.

- Acceptance

The Art Of Detachment

If you are not sure on what you should become or who you are.
Become more aware of what you were yesterday,
who you are today, who you will be tomorrow.

- You're Future Is Generated By Your Routine

The Art Of Detachment

I hope you never forfeit your laughter
so others will take you more seriously.
I hope when you cry it is only
because you look at how far you become.
I hope that your pain doesn't stop you from loving so intensity
and so unconditionally,
I hope that you never learn to generate your worth
with the validation of the people around you.
I hope that you know you can
have hard days and setbacks without it impacting
your entire view of your Self worth.
I hope you can express yourself with the worries of others.
I hope you never lose yourself at the cost of someone else's
perception of you.
I hope that you grow to be happy
and content with yourself for yourself .

- I Hope You Heal

The Art Of Detachment

When you tell yourself it is possible, it can be possible.
Everyday dwelling on your past, imagine you shift your mindset and tell yourself it is possible to be great, to be healthy. Even if you need to lie yourself into believing it, you eventually will generate a different mindset, and your mindset is everything. Train your mind to see the good within everything. The enjoyment you get out of life depends on the quality of one's thoughts. Thoughts become your words and your words become behavior, behavior becomes habit.

- You become what you feed your mind

The Art Of Detachment

Nothing Matters. | Nothing Matters!

There is a line separating the same word with completely different meanings. To one they are the same, to another they can differ the difference between the two. These words show the difference that perspective has. One being nothing matters in a negative manner and other being positive. If you change your outlook on a situation the entirety of it shifts. Your perspective on life will change if you change your mindset.

The Art Of Detachment

Be the reason someone feels heard, seen and loved.

- Spread good energy and it will follow you

The Art Of Detachment

Let Them Go,
stop chasing people who left.
stop trying to explain yourself to people
who don't get you.
Let them leave, this is not the time to grieve about people
that walked out of your life, people that don't deserve you.
They abandoned you, they left you, or they hurt you.
Why do you need them, you don't, they walked away.
They cheated you less than who you are
they played you to feel incompetent,
used and abused you dismissed your accomplishments.
It is easy to build walls but breaking them down is harder.
If you don't let go you will lose yourself and realize you are going to
become the very thing you despise.

The Art Of Detachment

I don't believe everything happens for a reason.
Most people would disagree but
I think you are able to give everything a reason.

The Art Of Detachment

You can not heal from your past,
if you keep pretending it doesn't hurt.

The Art Of Detachment

Healing isn't never reaching the bottom, or never feeling like things won't change, healing is making sure you feel every fuckin' emotion there is. Healing does not prevent you from feeling pain,
healing doesn't mean you won't have bad days.
Healing is knowing how to climb out of the bottom, to reach ground one out of a million. I say this because the journey of healing never stops. There isn't an end level. There isn't a roof within the game of healing, it goes on. Healing isn't never feeling pain, healing doesn't allow you to not fall back down, healing allows you to deal with it differently with the strength of understanding and acceptance
of knowing that things can and will get better.

- There is no roof to healing

The Art Of Detachment

Is is okay to miss someone,

It is okay to feel the way you are feeling,

It is okay to hurt.

You loved and yearn for someone and that is beautiful

but do not confuse who you miss with the person they have become.

The Art Of Detachment

I write my story down,
 because I imagine someone else might be where I was,
 in that moment someone else might be throwing their entire self away,
to gain an ounce of love.
Someone else might yearn for the short lived feeling they are not alone.
So know,
that you aren't alone.
But I like to think this book will keep our story alive
the good, the bad, and ugly.
And may you burn this book but,
my words will live till they no longer remember them.

The Art Of Detachment

I know they were supposed to hold you and love you and their arms were supposed to be somewhere you called home but ended up feeling more like a chore to them.

Just because their lack of strengths couldn't carry the weight of yours doesn't mean you aren't enough.

- You are enough, you are just looking in the wrong direction.

The Art Of Detachment

Begin to look at people as a energy source,
your whole perception will change.

- Practice this and it will help you deal with people accordingly

The Art Of Detachment

You may not see them suffer,
you may not see their hurt like they made you hurt,
but their biggest punishment is who they are.

Let them suffer by themself,
their best revenge is to walk away.
Soon enough they will realize
what they had, and that they will never get it back.

- The greatest revenge is losing you.

The Art Of Detachment

Your energy will always be louder in a quiet room
before you even utter a word,
your energy tells you more about a person, then anything.

- Your energy will always be louder then any words

The Art Of Detachment

I'm sorry your first heartbreak was from someone
that was supposed to love you the most
and couldn't love you the way you needed.

I'm sorry you had to play rolls in a play you didn't sign up for.
I'm sorry that you've now put up a barrier to those around you,
I'm sorry you make it hard to love you because you've been hurt.
But I hope you take that hurt,
and turn it into something great.
I hope you heal,
I hope you give yourself the love you need and deserve.

The Art Of Detachment

You deserve all the good things that are happening, and you deserve all the good that is coming.

The Art Of Detachment

Feeling lonely isn't a reason
to lower your standards.

- Make peace

The Art Of Detachment

If you keep accepting
an apology without change,
you allow yourself to be manipulated.

- Acknowledge the manipulation

The Art Of Detachment

"As you spend your time chasing butterflies, they fly away.
But if you spend your time building a garden they come to you"

- Dont chase people, they do what they want to do
  if they wanted to be here with you, they would.

The Art Of Detachment

You have to do what is best for you,
even when you don't want to.
You have to understand that what you tolerate and allow
is what you will get.
When someone shows you they don't care,
when they are hot and cold with you,
walk away, it's not going to feel good or be easy.
You have to, you can't continue to allow people to walk upon you.
It's not fair to you, it not even fair to them

The Art Of Detachment

And as you begin your healing journey from whatever it may be, there are three things you need to know.

1. A big part of healing is simply sitting with your emotions.

2. There will be tears and a lot of them,

3. And as you heal you will feel less triggered by people and events from your past.

The Art Of Detachment

Even though all the heartache and pain
through all the bad, you are still here.
You are turning that pain and hurt into something great,
you are making something out of it and
that is something to be proud of.

The Art Of Detachment

And as you are generating a new mindset, a new life.

You have to be ready for change, you have to be able to know

It will cost you your comfort zone,

your old life, friends and family.

But know that the people that truly care,

Will stand beside you.

You will learn who to keep with you and who to let go along the way.

The Art Of Detachment

There is always a sun after a storm.

I can not tell you the right way to heal or I can't even really tell you how to heal.

But more so of how you can be there, to be a better person for yourself.

The Art Of Detachment

They can't heal you.

They can't take your pain away but,

they can empower you every step of the way.

The Art Of Detachment

Maybe the people that walked away were only ever leading you back to yourself, and here you are okay on your own. You are growing, you are healing, you are adapting and reclaiming all the pieces you let them walk away with. Here you are not depending on another person to fix you. Here you are doing that on your own.

- Here you are healing

The Art Of Detachment

And as you showed me who you were,
why didn't I believe you?

The Art Of Detachment

Feel the pain, cry and scream, be angry.
But know you will see things clear
as this storm passes.
And know this storm will pass.

The Art Of Detachment

And as I sit here writing this for you,
there is no proper way to tell you how to heal,
because healing looks different for everyone, but if you take the time to understand such trauma, what it is,
why you are feeling this way.
Maybe there isn't a reason, you cannot pinpoint why. But when you can understand it you will eventually be able to accept this feeling, it won't be easy. You will hurt and it will take time but if you continue to practice this mindset, it will get easier.

The Art Of Detachment

*A renowned neuroscientist speaks on anxiety
in a mel robbins interview : to the people that struggle with anxiety.*

They say 80% of our brain is developed by the time we have lived our first five years of life. Most of the anxiety you feel is caused by early experiences i childhood that weren't worked through, which is now stored into your body an playing out within your life. You see your body doesn't lie but your subconscious mind does. The feelings you feel within your body we call anxiety, really is an alarm, being a fear response. Your anxiety gets bad becaus when you have that fear or a sense of an alarm you essentially get scared, and we as people want to know where it is coming from or why. When you can't understand that feeling your mind runs and your anxiety gets worse which can make you fall into a panic state we call *panic attacks*. You see most people overlook the power of a young one but our eternity of our life now and who you are , is built from the day you were born. So a lot of the ways you subconsciously deal with your emotions is from your childhood what you may have practiced subconsciously or were taught. This falls into the people that feel like they are addicted to negative thinking or stress, you are taking in that feeling or fear within your body and you've challenged that worry or stress tha you have channeled into worry so you don't have to feel it. The neuroscientist explains that it is a signal from your inner child and we ignore those thoughts and feelings, the man says "would you ignore a child at a grocery store?" Ther are times you struggle and you know you should show up for yourself and be there but you don't. You will come to realize that you are ignoring a part of yo that is essentially crying for

The Art Of Detachment

elp, and asking for support. The anxiety you feel is a state of alarm and as you dwell on that feeling you may start to feel afraid that you can't figure out a reason for the fear. This indescribable feeling we call anxiety will create more fear and worry, like a snowball effect. The neuroscientist says you can not just fix your thinking, because that fear is imprinted within you from your childhood. If you were to realize that tension, that fear is an alarm from your inner child, a younger version of you that wants reassurance" You are afraid. Why you may ask, because your amygdala recognizes something from the external world, that being your worries, that feeling creates change in your body, causing your heart rate to go up, but your anxiety is your intuition that is screaming to be heard, but a lot of us don't listen, maybe because we are afraid. Sometimes our intuition speaks on things and feelings we don't want to believe or hear. That can include change and change can be uncomfortable for most people.

The Art Of Detachment

Somewhere in between now and then

whiskey turned water,

a friday night out turned to a night in the gym,

Saturday turned into a book and coffee.

The beach turned from a party spot to somewhere clear,

validations turned to affirmations,

and somewhere in between now and then I healed

and healing turned into this book.

The Art Of Detachment

Remember this as you heal

Healing releases on you and only you.

People can help push you but at the end of the day it is you and only you. You can't rely on others to do the inner work.

There will be setbacks, relapse is normal.

Healing is to be free and clear from past trauma, practice letting go on the guilt that is weighing you down.

Healing causes misalignment healing isn't about fixing

It is about re-building the connection to who you truly are.

Patience is key to healing.

It takes time to build dysfunctional habits,

and it takes time to break them. You are healing, do not try to go back to your old self.

The Art Of Detachment

Sometimes leaving is the only option.
Sometimes leaving is the only way for
them to realize.

The Art Of Detachment

Healing your inner child
by forgiving the person
that was supposed to love you but let their pain
manifest into yours.

The Art Of Detachment

" Hurt people hurt people."

I was once a hurt person.
I don't like this quote, I know it can be true though.
Sometimes you have to take responsibility for the action you may or may not have wanted to cause.

And it fills me with sadness
But hurt people do hurt people,
Not intentionally, but it doesnt change that because you are hurting you hurt others. It seems like knowledge we all know but don't practice.

The Art Of Detachment

Be proud of yourself.

Be proud of how far you have come.

It is not self-centered or arrogant to celebrate your achievements

It is necessary.

Be proud of yourself.

Be proud of who you are.

Be proud of where you have come from

and be excited for how far you can go.

The Art Of Detachment

There is nothing wrong with you

Let the gentle words hug you and hold you in the darkest time,
let it be the reason you feel love.
There was never anything wrong with you.

- In a world so dark let these words be your light.

The Art Of Detachment

I won't forget the nights
I couldn't breath because I was crying so hard,
while begging for answers and to be healed
to be given the strengths to overcome this.
But I realized that the truth wasn't
for others to see the value in me but for me to see it for myself.

The Art Of Detachment

Healing is not becoming the best version of yourself, it is letting the worst version of yourself be loved, have the strength and knowledge to overcome those emotions and as your life will make you feel so depressed and outgrown maybe out of place until you have no other option but to make change. Remember healing is not linear, and it looks very different for everyone. Healing is growth and change, we are always growing and changing. Healing has no time frame, remember that.

The Art Of Detachment

And as you close this chapter,
let my name fade from the pages.
Let the distant memory fade as I put my pen down.
I plead for myself to not have use more ink writing a story
I don't want to write.
You can not have your name within my book
and hope for a different outcome.
Leave this chapter of life within the pages of this book.

I will go on writing a new story,
with new beginnings,
and a better ending.

- Closure

The Art Of Detachment

Acknowledgements

The Art Of Detachment, Isn't A Lesson Of Letting Go.
it is a lesson of understanding,
It is collection of poetry and quotes each sharing a story of
love, loss, substance abuse, mental abuse, childhood trauma
and healing in four sections.
This is my heart in your hands, this is my greatest heartache.
This is the most vulnerable parts of me,
this is me taking my experiences, my pain
and beliefs throughout my lifetime and using it to offer you a place
of comfort and to take these lessons to begin healing yourself.

I don't think I would be here without these experiences.
It helped me be an advocate to those people who are struggling,
giving the words I wish I had heard in darker times.
It is a lesson of being able to differentiate the definitions.
Able to accept your past trauma because you can come to terms
with understanding it. I plead that you heal from whatever
you struggle with. Understand you're not alone healing is a process
and it doesn't happen overnight,
take the lessons and the hidden messages within this book
live on with them. Thank you.

    - *Madison Farraway*

The Art Of Detachment

www.ingramcontent.com/pod-product-compliance
Lightning Source LLC
Chambersburg PA
CBHW021106080526
44587CB00010B/398